classic cottages
Simple, Romantic Homes

classic cottages
Simple, Romantic Homes

Brian Coleman
& Douglas Keister

Gibbs Smith, Publisher
Salt Lake City

First Edition
08 07 06 05 04   5 4 3 2 1

Text © 2004 Brian Coleman
Photographs © 2004 Douglas Keister

Published by
Gibbs Smith, Publisher
P.O. Box 667
Layton, Utah 84041

Orders: 1.800.748.5439
www.gibbs-smith.com

Designed by Cherie Hanson
Printed and bound in Hong Kong

Library of Congress Cataloging-in-Publication Data

Coleman, Brian D.
   Classic cottages : simple, romantic homes / Brian Coleman ;
photographs by Douglas Keister — 1st ed.
       p. cm.
    ISBN 1-58685-332-5
  1. Cottages. 2. Bungalows. 3. Small houses. I. Keister, Douglas.
II. Title.
  NA7571 .C596 2004
  728'.37 — dc22
                            2003022273

contents

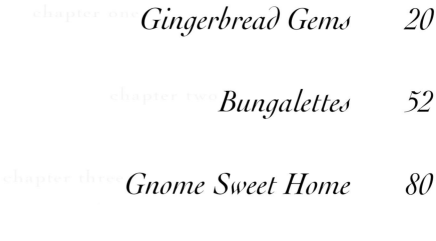

Acknowledgments

We would like to thank the following for their generosity and enthusiasm for this book.

Julie Castiglia

Sandy Schweitzer

Alana Coons

San Diego Heritage

Ed Zimmer

Denise and Keith Hice

Tropical Palms Resort

Stuart Echols

Forrest and Jeri Bone

Rick Meyer

Mark and Rhonda Gelstein

Allan Woods

The Shady Dell

Duke and Fay Waldrop

Vince Martinico

Library of Congress

Sarah Burkdoll

Dean Pederson

Kathleen Kelly

Richard Meyer

Joni German

Jennifer and Tom Wimperis

Doug McNaughton

Bill Peiffer and Ron Weber

Debra and Dave Byer

Bob Gravenor

Gordon and Gloris Johnson

Judith Bond

Deborah Brooks Pettry

Deborah Bodinger

Lucy Warren

Bill Cone

Sharon Hall

Bruce Du Chien

James Riley

Bill and Marilyn Strauss

Drew Hubbell

Nancy and Bill Knudsen

Steve Austin and Cathy Hitchcock

All the folks at Rejuvenation

Charlene Casey

Jane Curley

Lanny B. Brustein

A. Cascio

Ben Baltic

Paul Duchscherer

Introduction

Simple picturesque bungalows, quaint thatched stone and stucco huts, or elaborate marble and plaster palaces—all types of homes have been called a cottage. Loosely defined as any small, romantic dwelling, cottages range from nine-teenth-century gingerbread gems to quaint storybook châteaux to rolling bungalows of the 1930s. While their popularity for the last 150 years has never waned, cottages are now being rediscovered in record numbers as people look for affordable housing that is still

"A Cottage by the Side of the Road in Cape Cod. Mass." postcard embodies all of the charms of Cape Cod style, with a simple, appealing wood-shingled exterior painted a cheerful white with green shutters, surrounded by a white picket fence.

appealing and attractive. And as modern life becomes more stressful, the value of the peaceful home becomes even greater. What could be more relaxing than coming back to a rose-covered, romantic bungalow after a long day of e-mails and faxes, and gridlock on the drive home? For many, a picturesque cottage is exactly that—an escape to a simpler time, when life was slower, less complicated, and less worrisome. The simple and honest appeal of a cottage has also become more attractive as many empty-nesters downsize their homes and look for smaller but attractive alternatives to the large family house. Classic and timeless, cottages have never been in greater demand.

The Cape Cod cottage was first built by early New England settlers and was transplanted by missionaries to places as far away as Hawaii by the mid-1800s. New England values of frugality and hard work are echoed in the plain design of this cottage.

Cottages have been built since the Middle Ages but have not always been so appealing. Originally, cottages were plain, timber-framed buildings with one or two rooms that were crudely made, with high-pitched, thatched roofs. By the sixteenth century, these simple dwellings became larger and more attractive as they were embellished with oak-framed walls interspersed with stucco, stone, and small multipaned windows (because glass was so costly). Often surrounded by picturesque gardens, the romantic charm of these early Elizabethan cottages was popularized by Anne Hathaway, the wife of William Shakespeare, whose childhood home became synonymous with the idyllic charm of the English countryside. In the United States, our first indigenous cottage was the Cape Cod, a plain and unpretentious structure constructed by early Massachusetts settlers to withstand the strong gales of the seashore with its simple, low-gabled roof and lack of ornamentation.

By the middle of the nineteenth century, a major revival of historicism and romanticism began to sweep both England and the United States. Writers such as Sir Walter Scott brought back to life the glamour of the swashbuckling knights of the Middle Ages, while Henry David Thoreau extolled the virtues of living a simple life amidst nature. By the time Andrew Jackson Downing published his book Cottage Residences in 1842, people were already beginning to look for simple homes that could be built in romantic country settings, and it is no coincidence that Downing quickly became the cottage's leading spokesperson. Downing's new homes, "picturesque and easily executed," were just the right antidote for the more formal Federal and Greek Revival Neoclassicism that had been predominant for the past century. Downing instructed his readers that cottages were by definition more modest structures, "beautiful, rural, unostentatious, [a] moderate home of a country gentleman, large enough to minister to all the wants, necessities and luxuries of a republican, and not too large or too luxurious to warp the life and manners of his children."

Following Downing's success, other cottage pattern books were quickly published. Periodicals also joined the movement, such as Godey's Lady's Book, which printed designs for cottages in each issue, making hundreds of house plans readily available to the public. Developments from the railroads to the postal service made it easier and more attractive to live in the country in a picturesque home surrounded by gardens. This arrangement was the beginning of the modern suburbs.

More and more families began to follow Downing's advice, and it was not long before cottages in styles ranging from simple board-and-batten-sided structures to ornate Italianate cottage villas with bracketed rooflines and square towers, or campaniles, were being built. Little Gothic castles with crenellated rooflines, rusticated Adirondack cabin retreats of native stone and birch logs, even diminutive gingerbread-encrusted Queen Annes began to sprout

Anne Hathaway's cottage, actually a farmhouse, is the classic English countryside retreat. While life in such a cottage was quite harsh and conditions primitive during the sixteenth century, its romantic appeal has never waned. The picturesque gardens were not added until the early 1900s, replacing a muddy stable yard.

from coast to coast. The wealthy certainly did not want to be left out, so they built their own versions of the cottage as well, these being intended, however, for just seasonal residences, popularizing the concept of the cottage as a summer home.

Newport, Rhode Island, was one of the Gilded Age's favorite resorts, and by the latter quarter of the nineteenth century, summer cottages began appearing. But in reality, they were vast, opulent mansions. Cornelius Vanderbilt's The Breakers (1895) was one of the largest of these cottages—a seventy-room, full-blown extravagance of alabaster, marble, and mosaics designed by Richard Morris

Bungalows were big business by 1915, and just about everyone got into the act—even fruit packers. Who could resist "fancy, quality Bungalow melons"—especially if you lived in a bungalow?

Right: By the late 1920s Americans were singing the song of the storybook house—a romantic, quaint little cottage that was every couple's dream.

9664. Dick Turpin's Cottage, New Forest.

Dick Turpin was a famous eighteenth-century English highwayman who lived on the lam in this quaint Derbyshire cottage until he lost his temper and killed a neighbor's cockerel, resulting in his arrest and eventual hanging in 1739. Now you can rent the cottage for a unique, historic getaway.

Hunt in the Italian Renaissance style. Dozens of these summer palaces lined Newport's Bellevue Avenue, from the Gothic Revival Kingscote to the turreted Victorian Château-Sur-Mer, which featured a polychrome tower and elaborate Eastlake interiors by Richard Morris Hunt. All, however, were demurely described simply as "summer cottages."

By the early 1900s, the concept of the simple rural cottage had evolved into what was to become one of the most popular and enduring house styles of the twentieth century—the down-to-earth bungalow. Inspired by the Arts and Crafts movement, bungalows were by definition unpretentious dwellings in which craftsmanship was celebrated and an emphasis placed on honesty of construction and design. Bungalows varied in size but were often small, with only four or five rooms (parlor, kitchen, dining room, and bedrooms). Cozy and frequently centered on a fireplace, bungalows featured natural woodwork and built-ins, making them practical, economical houses to build as well as easily adaptable to locations across the country.

Newport, Rhode Island, 1895. Cornelius Vanderbilt's summer cottage, The Breakers, overlooks the ocean. It was only used for six weeks each summer during the social season.

The name "bungalow" originated from the Indian word bangla, meaning a house, and was originally used to describe barracks with overhanging eaves in British Colonial India. As the Arts and Crafts movement gained momentum in the United States, any single-story house with a low-pitched roof became a bungalow. In reality, many of these bungalows, especially the smaller ones, were just another of Andrew Jackson Downing's "simple cottage retreats." Affordable and easily available through mail order,

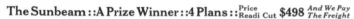

The Sunbeam :: A Prize Winner :: 4 Plans :: Price Readi Cut $498 *And We Pay The Freight*

A PRIZE WINNER designed to gladden the hearts of those who are looking for a small compact house of up-to-date appearance. It is astonishing to find so complete a home in such small compass and with so many conveniences at so low a price. The Sunbeam is made in four floor plan arrangements. They are all priced alike. The hood over front door is included in the price.

The price in single construction, specifications for which are given below, is **$498.** The price in double construction is **$595** and the specifications are the same as below except that the following materials are added: Sub-floor sheathing under finished floor with building paper between two floors, outside wall sheathing under bevel siding with building paper between, sash weights, cord, pulleys and locks for all double sliding windows and additional nails for this extra material.

Aladdin Homes sold prebuilt kits of modest homes guaranteed to "gladden the hearts" of purchasers—for under $500! (Courtesy Rejuvenation.)

Right: A Gothic Victorian cottage covered in climbing roses was the perfect old-fashioned holiday retreat in the early 1900s.

1506 - Rose Covered Cottage.

bungalow cottages rapidly became the most popular housing style in the country and remained so until the 1920s.

Following World War I, change began to sweep across the country as the returning soldiers, their minds still spinning from all of the new sights they had seen in Europe, were no longer satisfied with the straightforward simplicity of their Craftsman homes.

Prohibition had been passed in 1920 and then repealed in 1933, creating a social backlash that broke down old inhibitions and barriers and set the stage for a revolution in design. Americans had just finished saving democracy; they planned on enjoying themselves and were not about to let anyone stand in their way, including stodgy old Uncle Sam. Women led the rebellion, starting with the Nineteenth Amendment, passed in 1920, which granted them the right to vote. Hemlines were raised above the knees, corsets were tossed out, and hair was bobbed. Eddie Cantor belted out "Making Whoopee" from his Broadway hit as people listened to news about the latest wacky flagpole sitter.

Collecting Water from the Stream, 1892. Anne Hathaway's heirs had begun marketing her cottage as a quaint tourist spot in the bucolic countryside of England by the 1890s. One of Anne's descendants was still living in the cottage and gave tours through the 1890s.

Hollywood played a large role in setting the stage for the public's taste as well. When moviegoers began watching beautiful stars such as Gloria Swanson sweep down staircases of luxurious mansions, they began wanting to live in their own mansions, too, whether it was a Normandy château or a red-tiled Spanish hacienda. By the mid-1920s, fanciful storybook-style homes, loosely based on historic examples and inspired by Hollywood, were being built from coast to coast.

Not all of these were mansions, however. Many were simple cottages enlivened with an extra bit of decorative detail, such as exposed timber beams to imitate an English manor house or rough stuccoed walls made to recall an old Spanish mission. Smaller versions of the real thing, these storybook houses of the 1920s were just another take on the nineteenth-century romantic ideal of the classic cottage.

Henry Ford introduced the first Model T in 1908 for only $850, and it wasn't long before the entire country was clamoring for automobiles. This was also the beginning of buying on credit. Why scrimp and save when you could buy a new Tin Lizzie for a few dollars down? Millions did. Pressure from the public brought about improvements in the nation's roads, and by the mid-1920s, traveling in a "tin-can" and eating out of tin cans, these "tin can tourists," as some of the earliest auto campers were called, became an increasingly comfortable and affordable way for the average American family to vacation.

While the early auto trailers were simple structures, often with awnings that attached to the sides for more room, more durable styles were being produced by the 1930s, including Bread Loaves, Canned Hams, and Teardrops. The Bread Loaf design was a basic rectangle with curved edges ("straight from the bread pan") and the most efficient and economical to build. Curved with an arching roof and flat-paneled sides, the Canned Ham complemented the popular curvilinear style of automobiles of the times. The tiny Teardrop was the economical cousin of the Canned Ham, with its low roof leaving just enough room for two to snuggle inside. Influenced by the airline industry, streamlined Silver Palaces were produced by Airstream, making trailers in aerodynamic shapes that were comfortable, too. Interiors were outfitted as rolling homes, with all of the comforts—from tiny kitchens to upholstered walls and comfortable fold-down berths. Perfect for enjoying vacations that included the scenic outdoors, America's love affair with their "rolling bungalows" was a reflection of their affection for the simple cottage—and now you could bring it along with you.

This 1949 nineteen-foot Gypsy Traveler Vagabond trailer is appropriately towed by a 1949 Buick Sedan. Vagabond was founded in 1931 in New Hudson, Michigan. The name survives today as a division of American Recreational Vehicles. The trailer is photographed at the Tropical Palms resort in Kissammee, Florida, in front of a row of neo-bungalow cottages that were specially manufactured to give the resort the charming look of an old-time cottage court. Tropical Palms combines a classic cottage court with a campground for recreational vehicles.

Enclaves of cottages have been popular since Victorian times. Often intended just for summertime use, simple homes were often built in clusters in rural settings, and these rustic dwellings lent popularity to the concept of the cottage as a vacation retreat. By the turn of the nineteenth century, these enclaves were adapted for urban settings as courtyards of cottages, where groups of similar-style homes were built together around a central feature such as a fountain. Meant to provide privacy from the street, as well as a sense of intimacy, these cottage enclaves were most popular with bungalow and storybook-style housing.

Picturesque and inviting, the cottage harkens back to gentler times, a time when craftsmanship was celebrated. No matter how complex life seems today, the simple, classic cottage will always be waiting to welcome you home.

Opposite: The interior of the Vagabond is a fine example of tidy and efficient design. The warm wood surfaces combined with period accessories work perfectly to give the trailer the look and feel of a cozy summer cottage.

Savvy trailer manufacturers marketed their products as cozy cottages, perfect for a weekend getaway or a permanent home. This advertisement for a "cottage type" Fleetwheels trailer appeared in the May 1939 issue of *Automobile and Trailer Travel Magazine*. (Courtesy Leo and Marlys Keoshian Collection.)

chapter one

Gingerbread Gems

*V*ictorian architecture appeals to the imagination with its fanciful, whimsical designs and love of color and ornamentation. Not everyone, however, wants to actually live in a rambling Victorian mansion today. Difficult to maintain and costly to furnish, large nineteenth-century homes in the twenty-first century are often reserved for the few dedicated preservationists who have the interest and resources to restore and run them. In fact, many are turned into bed and breakfast inns. Many people have discovered that a "gingerbread gem," or petite Victorian cottage, is just the solution to their love of Victorian design. At a fraction of the cost, smaller and more practical Victorian cottages can still have all the appeal and charm of their larger cousins, but without the troubles a larger home demands.

Jacksonville, Oregon, Queen Anne, 1892. Built by wealthy Jacksonville merchant and miner Jeremiah Nunan for the then-substantial sum of $7,800, this was Design Number 43 in George Barber's popular book *The Cottage Souvenir.* Nunan bought the house as a Christmas present for his wife, and the cost included shipping, labor, and freight. A large redbrick chimney picturesquely projecting over the front facade, an asymmetrical roofline, and a turret all combine to give the cottage a wonderfully romantic quality.

Cottages first became a popular means of housing in the nineteenth century, initially as a reaction to all the changes society was going through at the time. By the mid-1800s cities were crowded, polluted, and impersonal. Beliefs once held as irrefutable were being challenged every day. Karl Marx called for equality, liberty, and revolution for the workman in his 1848 Communist Manifesto. Fossils were being uncovered and Darwin published his Origin of the Species in 1859. Abraham Lincoln signed the Emancipation Proclamation in 1863. For many people, the solution to all of this turmoil was to escape to a simple and picturesque cottage in the peaceful countryside.

Lincoln, Nebraska, c. 1885. This Eastlake home evokes the feel of an English cottage with its steeply rising gables and charming, arched balcony above the front entrance. A wide, curving veranda is an American touch. Late-nineteenth-century colors of rust, rose, and blue give the house a cheerful note and help accent the stick-style exterior detailing.

Mansard House, Amenia, New York, c. 1870. Mansard roofs originated in France, designed to create more living space on the top story without the appearance, however, of another floor, as taxes were based on the number of stories in the house. This diminutive example has the feel of a French mansion but on a smaller scale. Earth tones of buff, red, and blue follow Downing's advice to paint one's home in colors that were "harmonious with nature."

Methodist Campground, Oak Bluffs, Massachusetts, c. 1860s. Martha's Vineyard on the coast of Massachusetts has long been a favorite summer resort, and the Methodist Campground there was originally founded in 1835. The original tents were replaced by Carpenter Gothic cottages in the 1860s. Oops, the cottage on the left was built in 1867 and Hartease in 1864. Candy cane colors emphasize the cheerful, informal summer atmosphere of the camp.

Above: Aspen, Colorado, 1894. This mountain stick home is typical of cottages ordered by catalog and shipped to Aspen during its peak as a mining town in the late nineteenth century. Cheerful colors of blue and purple with yellow accents reflect Aspen's love of color.

Aspen, Colorado, 1883. A striking polychrome palette of twenty-five colors, including blues, greens, and oranges, sets off the entry to this mountain Victorian in Aspen. The body of the house remains more subdued, accenting the charm of this colorful cottage.

Opposite: Leadville, Colorado, 1904. Another colorful Colorado Victorian cottage, this type of building is called a "shotgun," or "tunnel," house, where the rooms were built one behind the other. If you wanted to, you could stand in the front door and shoot a shotgun out the back. Leadville was the home of Horace Tabor and Elizabeth McCourt Doe, also known as "Baby Doe." Tabor was a millionaire who made his fortune mining silver. Leadville is the highest city in the country, more than 10,000 feet in altitude. Note the steel chimney caps, a trademark of tunnel houses.

Cottages of the Victorian era reflected the major architectural styles of the period, many of which overlapped in times of popularity. Gothic Revival, popularized by Downing and his cottage pattern books, was the first style associated with Victorian cottages and was prevalent from the 1840s until the 1860s. Alexander Jackson Downing designed Lyndhurst in 1838 in Tarrytown, New York. It was considered America's finest Gothic home, and it wasn't long before pointed arches, prominent barge-boards with exaggerated Gothic tracery, tall arching windows, and steep gables were found on miniature cottage villas throughout the country.

As the interest in romantic styles broadened in the 1860s through the 1880s, the Italianate style developed, based on picturesque, crumbling

Columbus, Ohio, 1863. The Folly, as this house is named, is a national historic landmark as it is the only double, one-story octagon in the country. An earlier house on the site, built in 1830, was enlarged by Leander May, who constructed an octagonal addition around the original structure in 1862. Phrenologist Orson Squire Fowler's 1854 book *Octagonal Houses: A Home for All* started a short-lived fad for octagons across the country, as octagonal houses were reputed to be healthier than conventional homes, due to what was perceived as superior air circulation, as well as more efficient floor plans.

Lafayette, Indiana, 1893. Multiple gables, a wide veranda, and patterned shingles combine to give this Eastlake home all the charm and appeal of a romantic cottage.

Cape May, New Jersey, 1883. This charming, gingerbread-encrusted Gothic Victorian is highlighted by an ornately carved porch railing in the forms of circles, as well as scalloped verge boards. Cape May, one of only a handful of national historic landmark cities, is well known for its colorful collection of Victorian "painted ladies." These cottages were mostly built from pattern books of the 1870s and 1880s, after a large fire destroyed much of the town in 1878 and a frenzied rebuilding took place.

Italian villas, a favorite subject of nineteenth-century artists, often freshly inspired after making their grand tour of Europe. John Nash, the famous English Regency–period architect, is credited with the introduction of the style in England in the early 1800s. Queen Victoria herself gave her seal of approval to the romantic style and had Prince Albert add two square towers to their Italianate retreat on the Isle of Wight, Osborne House (1844–49). It wasn't long before the look was emulated in England. Campaniles (square towers), columned verandas, arched windows with pediment caps, corner quoins, and cupolas were incorporated everywhere, from urban row houses to elaborate countryside cottages.

Marysville, California, 1855. This Gothic cottage was the first brick building built in Marysville. The Aaron family lived here from 1874 until 1935, but it is now a museum for the city and Yuba County. The crenellated roofline accented by prominent spires gives the appearance of a romantic miniature castle.

Lincoln, Nebraska, 1878. The Lewis-Syford House, built in the French Second Empire style, is accented by a mansard roof cresting above the porch and large floor-to-ceiling windows that open out onto the porch from the front parlor. Built by Elisha M. Lewis, an early Nebraska pastor and missionary, the house was deeded in 1965 by the Syford family, its second owners, to the Nebraska State Historical Society Foundation. It is the oldest building on the University of Nebraska campus.

Seattle, Washington, 1905. This ornately decorated Victorian was covered in white vinyl siding when its owners began remodeling it fifteen years ago. A turret was added with the Latin motto *Quo amplius quo amplius* ("The more the better"), which sums up their philosophy. Details drawn from other Victorians around the country include hand-carved sunflowers, an owl, and a sea serpent—typically whimsical Victorian touches. Roof cresting was created from an antique cemetery fence, and griffins were added to the ends of the cresting.

Seattle, Washington, 1905. The Turkish Room in this Victorian cottage features a hand-painted Arabic frieze, an antique asymmetrical chandelier with colored shades, and Turkish paraphernalia, including a hookah pipe. The horseshoe-shaped entrance leads to the turret.

30 classic cottages

Pasadena, California, 1895. A transitional-style cottage with Queen Anne details applied to a Craftsman body. Note the pediment columns and scrollwork, classical touches masterfully integrated into the Arts and Crafts structure by the design sensibility of its well-known architects Charles and Henry Greene. The original owner's granddaughter, who has lived in the house since 1923, has spent her life preserving and restoring her home.

The reign of France's Napoleon III (1852–70) gave rise to the Second Empire style. Those with good taste in America followed the French lead in fashion and design, and houses were no exception. The most prominent feature of French homes, the mansard roof, was developed to allow more living space in the attic, and this was incorporated in American homes of the period as well. Elegant French interiors were adopted by the wealthy for their cottages in places such as Newport, Rhode Island. In reality, interiors were often imitations of French palaces such as Versailles. The Financial Panic of 1873, however, made such opulent lifestyles less secure, and by the late 1870s the French Second Empire style had rapidly fallen out of favor.

Charles Locke Eastlake published his influential book Hints on Household Taste in 1868. His suggestions for honesty in construction and simplicity of designs, which were often patterned on medieval English furniture, were translated in the United States into details such as

(Continued on page 37)

Ouray, Colorado, 1890. This cheerful cottage, built in a simple stick style, has been given a new life with a rainbow of bright colors, including barn red, sunshine yellow, and forest green. You can't help but smile when you walk by.

Opposite: Aspen, Colorado, 1882. This sweet little Victorian cottage was originally a miner's log cabin. The addition to the left of the house, made in the early 1900s, served as Aspen's first kindergarten. Cozy and colorful, this is the perfect rural retreat.

Black Hawk, Colorado, 1863. Built as a wedding present by tollgate keeper Lucien K. Smith for his bride, Mary Germain, the Lace House Museum was restored by the city of Black Hawk in 1976 for its centennial. The elaborate verge boards and a dripping confection of icicles emphasize the Gothic verticality of the home. Note the siding is laid vertically—a typical Gothic design. Gothic homes were popularized by A. J. Downing beginning in the 1840s and were fashionable until the 1870s.

Howell, Michigan, 1895. In reality, this exuberant Queen Anne cottage is, of course, a large and comfortable Victorian home. Barber and other nineteenth-century pattern-book publishers popularized similar cottage designs across the country. The word *cottage* is used to emphasize a home's picturesque and romantic qualities, no matter what its size. The owners of this period cottage used paint scrapings and old photographs to help restore their home to its original color scheme.

New Orleans, Louisiana, 1870s. This delightful single-shotgun cottage was built in a garden of the Faubourg Marigny, the site of the former plantation of the Count of Marigny and New Orleans' first suburb. The cheerful color scheme brightens what was formerly a sadly neglected home
before it was rescued and restored.

incised geometric borders, beveled corners, and insets of tongue-and-groove paneling. Japanese aesthetic embellishments such as fans or sunflowers were often added as well. Cottages built in vernacular forms incorporated these Eastlake details, and were also at times labeled "stick" style due to their linear forms. Popular from the 1870s thru the 1890s, Eastlake cottages often included deep projecting eaves supported by simple gable trusses and brackets, sawtooth cutouts in gable ends and porch railings, and, frequently, vertically applied siding that enhanced the home's design.

By the 1880s and until the turn of the nineteenth century, the eclectic, picturesque Queen Anne style was popular for everything, from humble

Algiers Point, Louisiana, 1892. This double-shotgun cottage in the historic district of Algiers Point (just across the river from New Orleans) was built for $1,800. The cottage became famous during its restoration on the television show *This Old House,* helping many other homeowners to visualize their restoration dreams.

New Orleans, Louisiana, 1836. An early cottage in New Orleans, this house was originally built by Asher Moses Nathan, a Jewish merchant from Amsterdam. Classical Greek Revival details, such as the exterior block siding, are combined with the form of a French Creole shotgun cottage. The vibrant paint scheme is reflective of the colors popular in New Orleans during the 1830s.

cottages to grand mansions. Inspired by the English, where the Queen Anne Revival developed in reaction to the more formal Gothic and Italianate styles, Queen Anne cottages were characterized by asymmetrical massing and rooflines, often accented by features such as turrets, tall chimneys, projecting bay windows, and generous decorative applications, from sunbursts and fans to ball-and-stick spindles above the porch.

By the end of the century, sparked by the 1893 Chicago World's Fair, interest began to turn away from the overly decorated styles of the Victorian era to simpler, classically inspired architecture, leading to the Colonial Revival movement and soon the bungalow.

New Orleans, Louisiana, 1855–1860. Built in the French Quarter, or Vieux Carre, of New Orleans, this shotgun cottage is a classic example of the style. Ornate spindles and brackets enliven the straightforward architecture.

New Orleans, Louisiana, 1871. The Casa de Felicidad was owned by two nineteenth-century dandies: Francois LaCroix, an artist and maker of coats and trousers, and Cordevoille, a duelist. Built between larger brick homes that dwarfed the little cottage, the Casa de Felicidad has been restored to its nineteenth-century vitality, and the home beckons with its simple charm.

Opposite: Cape May, New Jersey, 1872. The John Beniset House was built "on spec" by Peter McCollum in the late nineteenth century. The second owner named the Gothic Revival cottage Linda Lee for his daughter. Ornate brackets, corbels, and spindle work make this home a true "confection."

San Francisco, California, 1895. One's eye is drawn right up to the front door of this Queen Anne cottage with its striking circular fretwork. Ornately patterned shingles on the gable are topped by a beautiful crest—which goes to show, that no matter how small, any home can be accented with well-chosen details.

Top: San Francisco, California, 1893. This diminutive Victorian cottage in San Francisco's Western Addition is highlighted with a band of decorative detailing above the windows and acorns on the roof. It is details such as these that make a small house sparkle.

Selma, Alabama, late 1800s. This sweet southern cottage features a wide wraparound porch to take advantage of the breezes. Details such as decorative porch spindles and ornate fretwork on the gables give this charming house a touch of class.

The Lyford House, Tiburon, California, 1874. This turreted Second Empire cottage, accented with ornately carved gables, was built by Dr. Benjamin Lyford and his wife, Hilarita Reed, on land owned by her family, who were the largest landowners in Marin County. Threatened by development, the house was floated by barge to its present site in 1957 and is open to the public as part of the Richardson Bay Audubon Center and Sanctuary in Tiburon.

Left: Alameda, California, 1854. The Webster House is the oldest surviving house in Alameda, an island sanctuary of well-preserved nineteenth- and early-twentieth-century homes across the bay from San Francisco. This Gothic Revival delight looks like it is straight out of *Hansel and Gretel,* with its striking curvilinear decoration dripping from the eaves. Prefabricated on the East Coast, the house was shipped around Cape Horn and built on-site in Alameda.

Right: San Francisco, California, 1893. This Queen Anne cottage stands out with its wealth of exterior detailing, which is highlighted by the pastel polychrome exterior.

San Francisco, California, 1894. Once a boarding home for retired White Russian naval officers, this elegant Eastlake cottage is high-lighted with complex detailing accented with gold leaf.

Portland, Oregon. Ornate gingerbread embellishes the front porch entry, showing the owners' attention to detail. Note the beautiful stained-glass front door, created by a local Portland artisan after a period design.

San Francisco, California, 1890. You would not have recognized this fairy-tale turreted Victorian before its restoration. A previous remodel had added a second story to the building, but it was removed and a completely new turret was added for a more authentic and quite romantic look.

San Francisco, California, 1885. This well-proportioned, elegant Italianate cottage was built as part of a row of ten cottages, with a very narrow twenty-three-foot lot. A lovely pastel palette picks out the cottage's details nicely.

Portland, Oregon, c. 1890. This miniature Queen Anne jewel, sparkling with a wealth of gingerbread ornament and stained glass, is painted in a proper late-nineteenth-century autumn palette of greens, cream, burgundy, and gold, accented with a barn-red shake roof. But this house was not always such an eye-catcher. When the owners first purchased it nearly twenty years ago, it had seen more than its share of updating. Red composition siding with yellow trim covered the exterior, a Colonial Revival front door had replaced the original, and any traces of original gingerbread trim had long ago been thrown on the scrap heap. Bought for only $30,000, the owners planned to simply renovate the home and then resell it. But once they became involved in the restoration process, they found they were hooked, and rather than selling their Victorian cottage, they meticulously restored it and have now begun their own restoration business.

Opposite: Dramatically draped portieres frame the parlor and separate it from the dining room. It's hard to imagine the room twenty years ago, when 1950s linoleum covered the original hardwood floors and shiny high-gloss pink paint covered the peeling wallpaper. The current owners wallpapered the room twice, initially with an inexpensive burgundy paper, then again, several years later, with a sophisticated Brillion Collection frieze and wall fill in purples and greens. One of the owners hand-stenciled the intricate ceiling pattern himself—twice. After getting halfway through, he realized that the ceiling was not symmetrical and had to start over. The whole process took several years. Lit by an 1876 Cornelius and Baker chandelier, the room is furnished with Renaissance Revival furniture, including a tufted, medallion-backed sofa and a nineteenth-century burled-walnut piano (the owner enjoys playing jazz). An ebonized tête-à-tête beneath the chandelier centers the room.

The kitchen was kept intact and restored to the 1930s era. The owners didn't have the heart to rip out the 1930s tile backsplash in the kitchen, and so restored it to that period. Vintage appliances were found, including a 1930 Westinghouse coil-top refrigerator and a vintage range. A collection of colorful Jadeite dishware lines the glass cupboards.

Detail of the dining room showing the plate rail that holds a collection of Queen Victoria memorial china and portraits of the homeowners' ancestors. The Lincrusta dado was painted a rich burgundy and highlighted to give the appearance of old tooled leather.

A small eight-by-ten-foot second bedroom off the dining room was made into an office. Taking out the closet left just enough room for a Victorian recamier—button-tufted, of course. Serene swirls of chrysanthemums cover the walls; the hand-blocked, vegetable-dyed Morris paper was bought on a trip to London. Opaque stained glass was added to screen out the neighboring house, and one of the homeowners even hand-stenciled the window shade.

Rose Cottage, Los Angeles, Cal.

Rose Cottage, Los Angeles, California, early 1900s. This cottage featured a prominent, rose-encrusted front gable—a romantic view of the temperate West to send back home.

Opposite: The dining room is bathed in the light of a glowing stained-glass window of entwining irises, made by a local Portland stained-glass artist. This window was designed after windows in the Knapp Mansion, an 1875 Portland landmark now demolished. Ornate, jeweled, and stained-glass windows have been added throughout the house, based on designs by the Povey Brothers, Northwest artisans during the nineteenth century who were renowned for their windows (they designed the magnificent stained glass of Craigdarroch Castle in Victoria, British Columbia). Stylized irises continue in the frieze around the room, and the walls are papered with a Schumacher design. A Cornelius and Baker chandelier is centered above the Victorian black-walnut dining table.

chapter two

Bungalettes

U biquitous across the country during the first quarter of the twentieth century, bungalows were a truly vernacular housing style, conceived for the average American citizen. With prices starting at just $500, many bungalows were tiny—less than 700 square feet—and contained only a living room, kitchen, bathroom, and perhaps one or two bedrooms. The beauty

Seattle, Washington, 1925. This Mediterranean-style brick bungalow was built with bootleg gin profits by a crooked Seattle judge as a reward for a local police lieutenant who helped him supply speakeasies during Prohibition. Even the judge must have felt it was ironic that he was later arrested, caught smuggling the illegal hooch by a photographer from the bungalow's living room window! The house was still remarkably intact when the current owners bought it in 1981, and they only had to make minor cosmetic repairs.

The bungalow's interior still had all of its original mahogany woodwork untouched, and the owners simply painted the walls a dark peach. The original Batchelder-tile fireplace centers the end of the long living room, and is set off by arched, beveled-glass bookcases on each side with corresponding arched, stained-glass windows above. The owners have decorated the home as if the police lieutenant had just stepped out, with a typical 1920s mélange of exotic styles, from Mediterranean Revival furniture to Steuben art glass. The room is anchored by a period Wilton carpet.

of the bungalow lay in its practicality. Built-ins supplied extra storage; wide, overhanging eaves and front porches provided extra living space; and its clean and simple lines were a refreshing change from the formality of the Victorian era. Today, young homeowners are still attracted to bungalows for the same reasons as their grandparents. Practical and still economical to maintain, bungalows offer a maximum of living for a minimum of upkeep and cost. As young couples start out with their first home, often a simple small bungalow, or "bungalette," is the best choice not only aesthetically but economically as well. Small bungalows make it possible to have a home with style, warmth, and historical interest, and still stay within a budget.

Seattle, Washington, 1925. Detail of the 1920s sofa with its original upholstery that divides the long living room.

The dining room is furnished with more Mediterranean Revival furniture and a period chandelier. Lit by glowing Steuben art-glass shades, twin corner built-in cabinets hold a rainbow of Steuben stemware and dishes in iridescent golds, peacock blues, and soft pinks.

The master bedroom is furnished with a Neoclassical walnut bedroom set made by Berkey and Gay. An unusual 1920s Chinese-style chandelier, with hand-painted panels, dragons, and swags of beads, lends an exotic touch. Another period Wilton carpet with exotic birds and pagodas ties the room together.

Bungalows first appeared on the American scene at the turn of the nine-teenth century, an outgrowth of the Arts and Crafts movement that began in England thirty years earlier. William Morris built his Red House in a London suburb in 1859, designed by his architect friend Philip Webb. This home became the springboard for Morris's ideals of simple, honest craftsmanship, based on designs derived from nature. Morris's

The bathroom still has its original baby-pink tile work and fixtures. The owners recently completed a mural on the wall above of a shimmering underwater Art Deco design they copied from a period magazine.

Detail of the bathroom with its original built-in vanity cabinet, vintage lighting, and swirling Art Deco mural, which was added by the owners.

message spread to the United States and reached one of his most enthusiastic supporters, Gustav Stickley. A furniture maker, Stickley visited England in 1898 and after meeting many of the important figures in the Arts and Crafts movement, decided to open his own workshop in Eastwood, New York, in 1898.

Stickley also began publishing a magazine, The Craftsman, which was very influential in spreading the philosophy of the Arts and Crafts movement. The Craftsman included articles on everything from lifestyle advice to the appropriate furnishings for an Arts and Crafts home. House plans were available by mail from the magazine, made from drawings by

A 1932 Japanese pagoda birdcage held by a chain of swinging monkeys in a corner of the kitchen is a home to a singing finch named Caiaphas.

It seems like "Yes, We Have No Bananas," a song popular in the 1920s, should be playing on the radio as you walk into the 1925 kitchen. Original cream-colored cabinets, hexagonal drainboard tile, and the original cabinet pulls were all perfectly preserved when the owners moved in. They admit that the kitchen is what convinced them to buy the house. Vintage appliances have been added, including a 1930 coil-topped refrigerator that still runs without a hitch and a 1927 General Electric stove with a warming oven that is used every day.

Milwaukee, Wisconsin, 1919. This Tudor-Revival beauty brings to mind a miniature English cottage with exposed half-timbering and a stuccoed exterior. The owners took several years to decide on their historically correct color scheme, looking through period house pattern books and even analyzing paint scrapings. Their final choices were a period Colonial Yellow with dark green sashes and red trim accents. They added new brick-trimmed front steps several years ago in a period-appropriate design, as the original man-made limestone ones had badly deteriorated.

San Diego, California, 1910. The popularity of the Japanese influence is seen in the peaked gables of this colorful bungalette. The wing to the right is actually a new addition, a painting studio, that faithfully reproduced the original house's details for a sympathetic integration.

well-known architects such as Charles and Henry Greene. These plans helped popularize what soon became known as Craftsman-style bungalows throughout the country. Unpretentious homes, the smaller bungalows were frequently referred to as cottages.

Southern California, particularly Los Angeles, was the center for the construction of bungalows. As large sections of land were subdivided into the newly popular suburbs, developers and house plan books proliferated, offering modestly priced but well-designed, affordable homes. Sears, Roebuck and Company was one of the largest sources of bungalow plans, and in 1909 began selling entire homes by mail, precut and labeled so that a handyman could erect his own home for a very modest amount of money. Because of their ease of purchase, bungalows were built around the country, and nearly every city in the United States with new housing stock after the turn of the nineteenth century had bungalows.

Oakland, California, 1930s. Built by a local contractor, this Spanish Revival bungalow was one of a series erected on Monterey Boulevard in the 1930s. No matter that the home is only one story—the elegantly curved and proportioned entry makes it look like a grand Spanish hacienda straight out of Hollywood.

Oakland, California, 1930s. Another tract home built by the same builder on Monterey Boulevard, has well-proportioned details such as the divided chimney and a niche beneath, which make this bungalette an inviting Spanish cottage.

Bungalow styles can be broken down into a few different categories, although differences are not often significant. The Craftsman bungalow, originating from Stickley's Craftsman magazine and quickly adopted across the country, was the first and most popular style. Other variations included the Oriental bungalow, with gable peaks curved upward, imitative of the roofline of a pagoda; the Swiss bungalow with cutout railings and deep overhanging eaves; and, most often seen in the Midwest, Prairie-style bungalows with more angular lines and flatter roofs.

Craftsman-style bungalows were characterized by prominent peaked roofs that had deep projecting eaves and were supported by simple but substantial brackets. The gables usually did not have very steep pitches, adding to the horizontality of the bungalow's overall design. Overhanging rafter ends (rafter tails) were often cut into the ends of the roofline. Porches were wide, often the full length of the front of the house, and were supported by large, frequently overscaled but usually short columns in tapering trapezoidal designs that rested on wooden or brick piers, lending

(Continued on page 75)

San Diego, California, 1923. This inviting little bungalow has only had two owners since it was built by a local carpenter named Edgar B. Austin. The second owners bought the house from Austin's widow and were lucky enough to find all of the house plans and invoices in the home. Craftsman detailing includes the projecting porch roof supported by tapering columns set on brick supports.

San Diego, California, 1919. This Craftsman bungalow boasts oversized columns and a flat porch roof suggestive of a Prairie influence. Small yet inviting, this is another interpretation of the cottage.

Opposite: Oakland, California, c. 1905. Soaring Oriental gables give this little cottage great visual appeal.

Berkeley, California, c. 1905. A tiny bungalow with simple Craftsman detailing; its dormer window gives visual interest to the roofline.

Chico, California, c. 1915. As classic as American pie, the red, white, and blue color scheme of this bungalow is quintessentially cottage—charming, inviting, and picturesque. The wide overhanging roof and generous front porch are bungalow hallmarks.

San Diego, California, 1924. The homeowners painted their simple bungalow cottage the colors of a California sunset: Fired Orange, Waterworks Blue, Amber White, and Hunter Green. The owners repaired everything in the home—which had been used as a construction office and rental property before they purchased it—from the fireplace tiles to holes in the floor, but luckily, the building was still structurally sound.

Right: San Diego, California, 1924. The kitchen was intact with the original pantry cupboards, one of which opens into a root cellar. The walls were returned to their original color of yellow after fifteen layers of paint were removed. An original redwood counter was even revealed after linoleum was removed. A friend painted a trompe l'oeil window above the range of a view looking out over Point Loma, which is actually the scene that would be visible if a real window existed.

Opposite: Chico, California, 1925. The current owner's parents bought this charming Spanish Revival cottage when they were married in 1927, and their family has lived here ever since; she still enjoys her "basic little cottage." A rear patio was enclosed and another bedroom and bath added, but otherwise the house has remained unchanged, with details such as the original hardware and woodwork still intact.

Honolulu, Hawaii, c. 1910. Charles William Dickey (1871–1942) was one of Hawaii's most influential architects of the late nineteenth and early twentieth centuries. Dickey strove to develop an architecture suitable for Hawaii's climate and designed houses to show that the "culture of the people has asserted itself." Dickey felt that Hawaiian houses should have large windows and small wall spaces to let the tropical breezes and trade winds circulate. Porches with wide projecting eaves were also employed to protect against the frequent showers without needing to shut the windows. The wide projecting eaves added at a shallower angle from the main roof, called a double-pitched roof, became a trademark known as the "Dickey" or "Hawaiian" roof. Here Dickey's home looks out toward Diamond Head in the distance.

Piedmont, California, c. 1925. Stuccoed walls and an angled parapet roofline give this bungalow a Mission Revival look. The front porch is unusually placed on the diagonal, giving the little cottage a dramatic entry, which is accented by the thick, rectangular, overscaled columns.

San Diego, California, 1924. This classic Craftsman bungalow has a Neoclassical touch of round pillars on top of the square porch columns. The current owners did a paint analysis to determine their choice of the historically accurate colors of Sherman William's Colonial Revival Yellow, Colonial Revival Green Slate, and Roycroft Vellum. It was a simple two-bedroom bungalow when first built, but a third bedroom was added in 1935. Original built-in bookcases, a fold-down desk in the living room, and a dining room sideboard are all still intact, adding to the cottage's comfortable charm. The owners' renovation has sparked others in the neighborhood to do the same—a sure sign of a successful restoration.

Milwaukee, Wisconsin, 1922. Originally built for Miss Alma Deuster, the unmarried socialite daughter of Peter Victor Deuster, publisher of the Milwaukee German newspaper, the *Seebote,* Miss Deuster never actually lived in the home. Designed by Dudley V. Canfield, a local draftsman, this whimsical bungalow harkens back to the English cottage with its simulated thatched roof, windows and doors accented with brick, and white-washed stucco exterior. The home has had at least fifteen owners over its ninety-year history but has not lost its charm and quaintness.

Marin County, California, 1920. Everything is in harmony in this exquisite bungalow. The current owner has meticulously restored every aspect of the home, turning it into a showcase. When first purchased, the home had been updated with metal windows and sliding glass doors. The owner returned the exterior to stained shingle siding and wooden windows. The interior was taken down to the studs, walls were replastered using turn-of-the-century techniques, woodwork was replaced with handpicked quarter-sawn oak, and vintage decorative tiles were added in the baths and kitchen. The owner's extensive collection of vintage lighting is a highlight of the home.

The parlor is centered on a quarter-sawn oak fireplace that holds a collection of Rookwood, Roseville, and other art pottery, and a signed early-twentieth-century German clock. The settle is a period Arts and Crafts piece and is unusual for its diminutive size. The hand-hammered inlaid Limoge copper box on the coffee table was done by Handley, a prominent Liberty and Company artist. Lighting is all Handel.

an air of solidity and mass to the front facade. Natural products were emphasized—wooden shingles were the material of choice for both the siding and the roof, while river rock and brick, either solid clinker brick or a brick veneer, were popular for bases of porch columns, foundations, chimneys, and fireplaces. This chapter focuses on examples of smaller-style bungalows, bungalette cottages that, as period ads proclaimed, were perfect for the newlywed couple or a young family.

Arts and Crafts sensibility was not to last much more than a generation, however. By the 1920s social changes began to sweep the nation, and bungalows were increasingly forgotten in favor of new, more colorful storybook-style homes as the country began to escape into the fantasyland of Hollywood and the movies.

Opposite: Lit by an Arts and Crafts chandelier, the dining area is furnished with a table by Gustav Stickley. Tiffany candlesticks and a Rookwood vase rest on the table. Paintings by early-twentieth-century artists hang on the walls.

Marin County, California, 1920. The master bath is seen through the dressing room off the master bedroom. Centered on a splendid Tiffany "ball" fixture, tiles were hand-designed to repeat the colors and pattern in the chandelier. The dressing room is lit by a Prairie-style chandelier. The chair is adapted from a Frank Lloyd Wright design. Notice the inlaid walnut edging in the floor—this was taken from a similar pattern in the owner's childhood home and used throughout the bungalow.

A splendid early-twentieth-century chandelier is centered above the kitchen table. New quarter-sawn oak cabinets, designed in a sympathetic Arts and Crafts manner, are highlighted by a collection of signed tiles from the California Tile Company, dating from the 1920s. Period stained glass was added to the window.

Marin County, California, 1920. Sunlight streams into the stained-glass windows in the bedroom. The side-table light is by Charles Parker, while the wall sconces are Louis Sullivan originals. The bed is a reproduction Arts and Crafts model with a custom woven Viennese bedspread of a 1906 design. An original Stickley rocker rests nearby.

Pasadena, California, 1914. The Reverend Cornelius N. Webster had this classic bungalow built for him from a plan book at a cost of $2,700. The house was shaped around the needs of a reverend, with doors to close off rooms so the congregation could visit and not disturb his family. The exterior was restored by the current owners, who replaced the elephantine porch posts that were damaged in an earthquake. Originally, similar posts lined either side of the driveway for a porte cochere. This sweet bungalow has become an icon, as it was selected by Encyclopedia Britannica to represent the bungalow in its online encyclopedia.

The bungalow's interior has been lovingly restored—wainscoting and woodwork were stripped and restained, and the house was furnished with period Arts and Crafts furnishings. There are twelve pieces of Gustav Stickley furniture in the living room alone, along with Van Erp vases and other period pottery.

The bungalow's study is highlighted by an original stained-glass piano window, meant to provide light above an upright piano. The wooden battens on the walls had been removed by previous owners but were replaced. More Stickley furniture fills the room. The owner was fortunate to begin his collecting more than twenty years ago, when Stickley was considered "old oak," and a chair or table could be found for $25.

Cobble Stone Bungalow, Orange, Calif.

A period Aladdin Homes catalog depicts children playing in front of a sweet Cape Cod cottage, its garden brimming with colorful hollyhocks in an irresistibly romantic image. (Courtesy Rejuvenation.)

This unusual all-cobblestone cottage in Orange, California, speaks to the rustic appeal of the bungalow.

chapter three

Gnome Sweet Home

*R*omance is on the upswing. Home and hearth are increasingly on many people's minds as their lives become more complicated. Many seek respite from their busy and stressful workdays in the comfort of their homes. And what could fit the bill better than a romantic storybook cottage? Whether it is a miniature turreted French Normandy château in New Jersey or a faux-thatched Cotswolds farmhouse in California, storybook-style cottages offer a historic appeal that is hard to duplicate. Still stylish after eighty years, these picturesque cottages are being rediscovered by a new generation of home buyers who find that you can live in an attractive smaller home with old-world style and charm, and forget about the boss until Monday.

Hollywoodland, California, 1930s. Hollywoodland was a development in the hills northwest of Los Angeles begun in 1923 by local builders. Soon its steep, winding streets were filled with miniature French Normandy castles, English cottages, Spanish haciendas, and other whimsical homes. Actors from Humphrey Bogart to Gloria Swanson bought picturesque cottages here. All the elements of storybook charm are seen: stuccoed and half-timbered walls combined with rubble stone accents, a prominent rubble stone-and-brick chimney, a seawave-pattern roof made to imitate thatching with jerkinhead gables, and diamond-paned mullioned windows with shutters.

Storybook-style homes originated after World War I as the popularity of the bungalow began to wane. Many returning American soldiers had been excited by the sights they had seen in Europe, including the half-timbered cottages of the English countryside and the turreted white-washed farmhouses of France and Belgium. Hollywood got in on the act as well, casting their stars in exotic mansions based on a variety of historic styles ranging from French châteaux to English country mansions. By the mid-1920s, homes were being built in a variety of storybook styles. Most of these homes were picturesque and petite cottage versions of the larger European originals.

English manor houses were a frequent source of inspiration. Some of the features found were half-timbering interspersed between rough-cast stucco; wood-shingled roofs, sometimes applied in an undulating fashion referred to as "seawave" patterning; jerkinhead gables; and small diamond-paned windows. True to Hollywood's influence, it was the look of Medieval

Albany, California, 1920s. Steeply pitched rooflines make this picturesque cottage seem larger, as does a tiny dormer peeking from behind the front porch gable. Typical of storybook homes, a mixture of styles and details, including Neoclassical swagged ribbons above the arched Spanish-style front window, give this small home an eclectic charm.

Milwaukee, Wisconsin, c. 1925. This whimsical English cottage à la bungalow is a showstopper in its neighborhood of more traditional bungalows. An exaggerated front porch, half-timbering on the upper gable, and a prominent projecting front bay make this house appear straight out of an English fairy tale.

Del Mar, California, c. 1925. This cottage could be in England as easily as southern California. The simulated thatched roof, white stuccoed walls accented by mullioned windows and shutters, and even the white picket fence all give storybook appeal to this perfect little cottage.

Oakland, California (Normandy Gardens), c. 1926. Contractor R. C. Hillen worked with architect W. W. Dixon from 1922 to 1926, publishing *The Home Designer and Garden Beautiful,* a magazine of storybook house styles of old-world architecture. Hillen built a picturesque tract of these homes in Oakland, each with a different facade but many with similar floor plans. This home references a castle, with its unusual crenellated roofline, exposed timbering on the upper gable, and prominent turret for English-country-house charm.

England that was the objective, not a direct re-creation, and so any artificial means available were routinely used to age materials and give them the look of true antiques. Timber beams were charred and distressed, windows and doors were proportioned to make them appear out of scale and more picturesque, and medieval-looking hardware elements were finished with antique patinas.

Vernacular French farmhouses were also popular: turrets interspersed with tiny arched windows; irregular courses of clinker brick or stone combined with whitewashed plaster or stucco; overscaled chimneys; and whimsical wrought-iron accents, from door hardware to balcony railings, began to sprout on miniature French Normandy cottages across the nation.

Honolulu, Hawaii, c. 1930. An English cottage in Hawaii? Why not? This rambling storybook cottage is surrounded by palm trees in Hawaii, but still looks as romantic as if it were in England. All the classic details are here that make storybook houses so charming: a catslide front porch roofline, exposed half-timbers, dovecotes on the gables (purely decorative, of course), diamond-paned windows, and English boxwood hedges lining the front lawn.

A detail of the roofline shows the whimsical touches that make this such an appealing house, from irregular exposed beams (newly made to look old and roughly hewn) to a tiny window in the gable with its own miniature roof and diamond-paned glass. The oddly shaped window in the other gable is pure Hansel and Gretel, shaped irregularly to appear handmade and worn with time.

The Spanish hacienda was another storybook style reinterpreted as a cottage. Rose-tinted stuccoed walls accented by thick beehive chimneys, red-clay-tile roofs, and extensive use of decorative wrought-iron elements were frequently found. Popular in warmer climates, Spanish Revival storybook houses were most frequently built in California.

(Continued on page 92)

Los Angeles, California, c. 1925. Two grand turrets distinguish this French Normandy cottage. An unusual wood-shingle roll-wave roof sets off the house and accentuates its storybook appeal. Wonderful clipped yew hedges frame an arch over the entry gate—what could be a more romantic entrance?

Albany, California, c. 1925. Storybook homes frequently used circular turrets for the entry, as first impressions are the most lasting. This example provides an interesting visual counterpoint to the rest of the one-story home and makes the entry seem much grander. Tiles provide a nice accent around the top and help break up the mass of the turret.

Oakland, California, c. 1925. A rose-tinted, red-tiled Spanish cottage brings back all the charm of the Southwest. The prominent beehive chimney studded with sandstone boulders is a handsome accent, as are the scalloped entrance arch and recessed living room window. The meandering front steps and front yard retaining rocks are original to the house.

San Diego, California, 1925. Built by Lewis Dodge, this modest Cape Cod cottage was nearly uninhabitable when its current owner bought it four years ago. A leaking roof, ancient plumbing, rotted windows and woodwork—even rats' nests in the walls—did not deter the owner, who was attracted to the original detailing still intact, such as mahogany trim, glass doorknobs, and original bathroom fixtures. The location, nestled among trees in a secluded canyon, was also an attraction. The owner researched the builder and even found his ninety-year-old son, and her efforts paid off as the house was awarded historic designation by the city of San Diego. The original simple shingle siding emphasizes the Nantucket cottage feel of this sweet home. Future plans are to replace the roof with wood shingles in a seawave pattern, based on pictures of the original.

Opposite: Oakland, California, c. 1925. Another of R. C. Hillen's cottages, an unusual pentagonal turret to the side of the entrance balances the upward sweep of the main front gable. Notice the tall chimney stack on the side of the house—a favorite storybook touch, using exaggerated scale to emphasize quaintness and charm.

Spokane, Washington, 1930. An exaggerated, massive front gable sweeps down to the ground with a red-ceramic-tile catslide roof in this imposing cottage. Red pressed-brick veneer covers the exterior and is set off by the fine terra-cotta front door surround. The asymmetrical design and prominent chimney in the front emphasize the look of an old English manor house. The interior is as well preserved as the exterior and features original woodwork, light fixtures, a wrought-iron and mahogany balustrade, and details such as a telephone nook in the first-floor hallway. The house was reputedly designed by the first owners' son as a class assignment while in college back East at a prestigious university.

Eagle Rock, California, 1923. Built for an eccentric German American named Baasch, this striking English cottage was added onto an original Victorian farmhouse on the hillside site. The grounds are highlighted by a dramatic arched entrance gate of stone and stucco that echoes the stone-and-stucco chimney of the main house above. Actors Matt Damon and Ben Affleck lived here at one time.

Spokane, Washington, 1929. The Cunningham house was designed by local architect Randolf Smith in a classic picturesque style. The ivy-clad stuccoed walls are accented by the red-tile roof with a jerkinhead gable. This cottage looks like it has been there for centuries—just the effect storybook builders aimed to create.

The stock market crash of 1929 and the Great Depression were not the end of storybook style, as might be assumed. Escapism was more popular than ever during this period, in the movies and in people's homes as well. Historically based, romantic storybook cottages remained in vogue until the 1930s. By then, however, Roosevelt's New Deal had been passed, and as the WPA began constructing buildings across the country, the new Streamline Moderne style replaced older, historically based designs of the 1920s. Americans began preparing for another world war, and most wanted to look to the future, not the past, for their inspiration.

Glendale, California, 1929. The year was 1929, and "The Great White Hope," Jess Willard, was at the peak of his popularity. Willard won the World Heavyweight Boxing title in 1914, beating the black heavyweight champion Jack Johnson after only twenty-six rounds in humid Havana, Cuba. It was a little difficult to stage the fight, as Johnson was on the run from the feds for "the importation of women for prostitution," and the fight could not be held in the United States. After Willard beat Johnson, his popularity was assured and "The Great White Hope" became a subject of movies and books. The phrase reflected the popular sentiment of the time: that is, the search to find a white champion to upset Johnson, the black and unpopular but reigning world heavyweight champion.

Willard had this French château-style cottage built with just one story but with all of the latest designs: Batchelder tiles around the fireplace, arched leaded-glass windows throughout, inlaid hardwood floors, colorful art glass, metal chandeliers, and wall sconces.

When the current owners bought the house in the early 1990s, it had had only four previous owners, and the original features were still intact. The light fixtures had never been altered, original plumbing fixtures were still in the baths, tiled in cobalt blue and mint green, and the mahogany trim throughout the house had never been painted. The owners only had to do cosmetic work, except for the roof, which they restored to its original seawave pattern using composition shingles to adhere to fire codes.

Detail of the end of the front gable. Intricately designed, hand-cut composition shingles were applied in a complex seawave and multipatterend design to emulate the original roof. Copper flashing beneath some of the shingles is one of the details that highlights designs such as the heart motif seen here.

Tucked cozily between the two wings of the home, the entrance turret centers the front of the house. The turret is accented by a second miniature gable in its roof, topped by a weather vane of a graceful angel in flight. Notice that the original hanging wrought-iron porch light is still intact. The owners painted the originally pink exterior in a soft Dove Grey trimmed with teal accents. The front courtyard is enclosed by a border of river rock and a rustic picket fence, both of which the owners added, stained to match the trim of the house. Notice the deeply inset windows, which retain their original leaded glass.

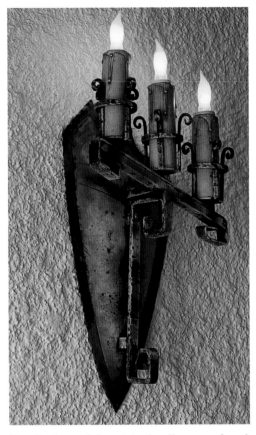

Detail of one of the original wall sconces found throughout the house. The colorful painted metal is in remarkably good condition and lends an appropriate note of period medieval charm.

The breakfast nook, the owner's favorite spot, is accented by a domed ceiling covered in roughly patterned plaster. The chandelier with its art-glass shades is original to the room. Arched leaded-glass windows with mahogany trim let light stream into the room. The kitchen table and chairs are from the 1930s, again passed down in the owner's family.

Elegant plaster-covered wooden pillars flank the entrance to the living room, which is still lit by the original polychrome wrought-iron chandelier. The fireplace boasts Batchelder tiles of a forest scene. The furniture belonged to the owner's aunt and uncle, and dates from the 1930s—exactly what would have been found in the house originally. There is even a period Victrola in the corner that still works but takes a bit of elbow grease to wind.

San Diego, California, 1925–26. This diminutive cottage is a charmer with its mullioned, arched glass front door, window boxes beneath double-hung windows, prominent chimney bisecting the front gable as if it were a grand English manor house, and a varied roofline complete with an eyebrow arch and a steep but tiny gable. Built by Frank Melcher, a local builder and realtor, the cottage has been the starter home for many young families, from teachers to navy seamen, who often outgrew its cottage proportions and moved to larger homes. Luckily, many of the original interior details remain intact, from blue-and-white hexagonal tiles in the bathroom to a niche above the fireplace for a special piece of pottery. One of the more unusual features that still remains is a drawer bed in the living room. A large drawer pulls out to reveal a three-quarter-size bed that tucks into a walk-in closet in the bathroom when not in use.

Pasadena, California, 1928. Casa de Pajaros sits in a secluded glen above the city and was the obsession of its owner for more than twenty years. Herman Koller began building his dream house in 1928, and continuously searched for stone, tile, and wooden fragments that he then incorporated into his unique stone cottage. The large arched front window helps impart a Mediterranean Revival look. An impressive entry gate built with a flagstone arch (not visible) sets the stage for this dramatic dream house.

La Jolla, California, 1928. Designed by a woman architect (quite unusual for the time) who was also married to an architect, this ivy-clad cottage suggests Elizabethan England, with its pointed gable and shingled roof meant to imitate thatching.

San Diego, California, 1905. The Strong House was built for William Hugh Strong, whose descendants still occupy it. The architect was Emmor Brooke Weaver, a prominent architect originally from Iowa. Natural exposed woodwork, simple whitewashed walls, and diamond-paned windows set beneath the steeply pitched overhanging roof all recall the best of the vernacular English Arts and Crafts cottage. A pergola at the right of the house was enclosed in the 1920s. The interior, larger than it looks from the outside, features dark woodwork and beams highlighted by light-colored walls, numerous built-ins, and rare original burlap insets in the dining room wainscoting.

Chico, California, 1928. A white picket fence neatly frames this storybook cottage that evokes memories of Normandy's stuccoed farmhouses in rural France. Located in Eastwood Park, an enchanted enclave of more than three dozen storybook-style homes built by developer Orville Tracy between 1925 and 1929, each home was unique. Priced between $5,000 and $9,000, a substantial sum for the times, Tracy hoped to attract wealthy doctors and professors from the nearby hospital and Chico State University. The entire neighborhood has been included in Chico Heritage Association's survey of historic buildings.

The front door was painted by the cottage's current owners as a tribute to Jackson Pollock, their favorite American artist. True to Pollock's Expressionist style, the door was taken off its hinges, laid flat on the ground, and dribbled with colored paints.

Opposite: Chico, California, 1925. Double gables set the scale and balance the two-story chimney of this English-style cottage. The house gives the impression of hand-built brick but is actually covered with a brick veneer at a fraction of the cost—a common storybook approach. The current owners maintain handsome plantings in the front that enhance the cottage's appeal.

The covered side porch is a new sympathetic addition by the current owners. Antique bricks accent the arched doorway; note how the stucco work of the addition matches that of the original house exactly.

Opposite: Chico, California, c. 1930. Favorite storybook motifs, including a catslide roof, exposed half-timbering, and a random brick design in the chimney, are used in this immaculate cottage. The interior was restored to a period English-cottage look, preserving details such as built-in cabinets with cedar-lined drawers, a built-in buffet in the dining room, and an arched ceiling in the living room. The owner loves roses, growing more than eighty varieties in her yard, and has now appropriately named the house Rose Cottage.

Chico, California, 1929. Said to be the crown jewel of developer Orville Tracy's Eastwood Park development because it had the steepest roof, this Hansel and Gretel cottage looks like it was built for a Hollywood set. The steeply pitched roof provides space inside for a sixteen-foot-tall living room, as well as two upstairs bedrooms and a bath. When the current owners bought the house, it was painted yellow, and they returned it to a more dignified gray with a vibrant red front door. Rough, irregular plaster walls, original mullioned windows, and some of the original hardware and fixtures inside are all part of this cottage's charm. Note the deeply recessed front entrance accented by the catslide front gable roof, which enhances the curbside appeal.

Pasadena, California, 1904. Busch Gardens was a large public garden maintained by brewer Adolphus Busch. It contained several storybook-style structures, including this thatched English cottage. The gardens were closed in 1938 due to funding problems, and the land was subdivided, though several of the original buildings still exist.

Milwaukee, Wisconsin, c. 1929. Picturesque ashlar stonework defines the rustic French-château look of this rambling cottage. A multi-gabled roofline punctuated with dormers adds to the appeal.

Exposed wooden trusses in the parlor and a dramatic barrel-vaulted ceiling highlight the interior of the home. The effect is country French château.

chapter four

Rolling Bungalows

America's Homes on Wheels

Two of the hallmarks of cottages are compactness and informality. Add a couple of wheels and you have one of the icons of mobile America—the travel trailer. The genesis of these models of efficiency was the Conestoga wagon that, loaded down with all of a family's possessions and pulled by a team of sturdy oxen, provided a temporary home for thousands of pioneers as they made their way west. These hardy pioneers, of course, abandoned their mobile home and settled into more permanent abodes.

It doesn't get much more modest than a teardrop trailer. This fine example, built from the bottom up by Bill Eosel of Port Sydney, Ontario, Canada, is towed by a 1948 Pontiac Streamliner Deluxe with a 248-cubic-inch Straight 8 and a four-speed hydromatic transmission, owned by Allan Woods, also from Ontario. A rarity for teardrops, this trailer sports a bathroom complete with shower, which pops up from the black steel box on the front of the trailer.

This sales brochure, dating from the late 1930s, for Schult Luxury Liner trailers touts the versatility of their rolling homes. Although Schult was promoting their trailers as recreational vehicles as well as residences, their boxy bread-loaf design suggests that they were more suited in a permanent mooring than gliding down the highway. (Courtesy Milton Newman Collection.)

This postcard from the 1930s aptly illustrates the transition from trailer court to cottage court. Although some cottage courts still exist, most of them have evolved into motor hotels (motels).

When this advertisement appeared in the June 5, 1937, issue of the *Saturday Evening Post*, Arthur Sherman's Covered Wagon Company led the trailer industry, having pioneered the affordable hard-sided bread-loaf trailer. This advertising copy compared the Covered Wagon to a five-room house that was perfect for "tourists, family vacationing, sportsmen, traveling salesman, engineers and army officers, show people, invalids and retired couples."

Interestingly, despite their long, adventurous journey, most of these pioneers, like other Americans after unloading their wagons and settling down, rarely ventured more than a few miles from their homes—that is, until a very important event occurred at the beginning of the twentieth century: the widespread popularity of Henry Ford's affordable automobile. The Model T and the eight-hour workday gave Americans the ability to exercise their treasured constitutional right of the freedom of movement (liberty); it gave them time to travel. But when folks hit the road in their Tin Lizzies, they found few places to stay along the way. So, the crafty travelers fabricated all manner of devices to attach to the automobile to provide them with a temporary sleeping shelter, including tarpaulins, wood and canvas lean-tos, tents, and bedboards that stretched across car seats. By 1919 there were enough of these mobile Americans to form organizations like the Tin Can Tourists, whose name described the tin-can provisions they carried with them. Eventually, a few clever folks attached tents to artillery-style trailers—a towable home on wheels—and the travel trailer was born.

In Bisbee, Arizona, the Shady Dell Trailer Bed and Breakfast offers overnight guest lodging in a choice of eight fully restored vintage trailers, ranging from a 1949 Airstream to a 1957 El Rey.

Although this Spartanette trailer qualifies as a house trailer because of its size, it comes under the heading of a canned-ham trailer because its ovid shape is reminiscent of the metal containers for packaged hams. The Spartanette was one of the sleeker Spartan brand trailers manufactured by Getty Aircraft, which changed their focus to more peaceful products after World War II.

Like all the trailers at Shady Dell, the Spartanette is furnished with period accessories such as a colorful glass-and-pitcher set, a 45-rpm record player complete with 1950s vinyl records, and the early RCA Victor portable television atop the counter. The sleeping area can be seen in the far background.

Enter one Arthur Sherman, a pharmacist from Indiana. Mr. Sherman took his family on a camping trip to northern Michigan in July 1928, with a newfangled "easy to set up in ten minutes" tent trailer. The Shermans arrived at the campground in a driving rainstorm and the ten-minute set up became a very long ordeal. Drenched and cold, Sherman was determined to figure a better way. During the next year, he tinkered with various devices and finally hit upon the idea of constructing a hard-sided trailer. His invention was little more than a box on wheels, but when he showed up at the campground the next year with family and

Photographer Marion Post Wolcott took this photograph near Fort Beauregard, Louisiana, for the Farm Security Administration in December 1940. While it may not have exactly fit one's image of a cottage in the woods, the $125 trailer did have the advantage of being easy to move to a more desirable location.

Perfectly constructed to provide a balcony-like view from its rear platform, this early 1930s custom-built trailer was constructed for the owner of a dairy in Canada. Prior to Arthur Sherman's Covered Wagon trailer, ownership of trailers, camping busses, and trucks (the predecessors of the modern–day motor home) was limited to the wealthy. Luminaries such as Henry Ford, Harvey Firestone, President Warren G. Harding, and Thomas Edison all participated in "auto camping" excursions.

Although this trailer lacks cooking and lavatory facilities, the interior is finished much as a fine home of the 1920s might have been, including parquet flooring, mahogany and gumwood paneling, and recessed panel doors. The windows roll down using automotive-style crank handle regulators; above each is a stained-glass panel. Early trailer interiors were generally fitted out by cabinetmakers who, lacking any other aesthetic precedent, simply followed popular domestic styles.

While a number of postwar manufacturers adopted a more fashionable leaning-into-the-wind silhouette, the New Hudson, Michigan-based Vagabond held to a conservative, bolt-upright design known in the trailering world as a bread loaf. This 1950 Model 262 (signifying a twenty-six-foot length and tandem axles) originally sold for $3,500 to $5,000 dollars, depending on options.

trailer in tow, he became the center of attention at the campground. He got so many inquiries about his boxy contraption that he decided to man-ufacture them. Dubbed the Covered Wagon by his children, Sherman's invention started a travel trailer boom that has never really subsided. Travel trailers begat house trailers, which begat mobile homes, which begat manufactured housing—but the towable and detachable travel trailer became and remains quintessentially an American symbol.

The heyday of the travel trailer was during the Great Depression of the 1930s, when Americans were on the move again, looking for jobs and a better life. This time, travel trailers, romantically referred to in the pop-ular press as "rolling bungalows," replaced the Conestoga wagon. They provided an inexpensive and portable home for hundreds of thousands of Americans. Indeed, travel trailers were so popular that in 1935 Wall

Above: A crosswise davenport, which converts into a bed occupying the forward end, has long been a staple of trailer interiors. Following a few years of experiment during the 1930s, interior arrangements soon settled into a fairly standard format. The living room, whose sta-tus was defined by the davenport, was placed at the forward end, with a main entrance door opening out to the right side. The kitchen/galley came next, while the sleeping area occupied the rear. The owners of this trailer rescued it from its mooring in the Sierra Nevadas in California, and lovingly restored and accessorized it to evoke a mid-twentieth-century charm.

A cleverly designed drop-down writing desk that could double as a small serving table overlooks a petite kitchen. The bathroom is behind the door on the left; at the rear is a bedroom with a separate entrance.

In 1934, a young couple purchased plans and hardware from the Hammer Blow Tool Company and built this trailer for their honeymoon. Like many trailers of the early 1930s, the Hammer Blow was essentially homebuilt. Manufacturers supplied the basic items like wheels, axels, frames, and hitches, and do-it-yourselfers following plans supplied by the manufacturer did the rest. The tow car pictured is a 1936 Oldsmobile, built by the onetime General Motors division based in Lansing, Michigan.

Right: Although the Airstream trailer has always been marketed as a travel trailer rather than a permanent home, it still has a lot of cottage-like charm. Its light weight enabled it to be towed by just about any vehicle, and its durable aluminum "skin" assured the sort of longevity that is usually reserved for homes. This 1936 Airstream Clipper carries the earliest known Airstream serial number. The tow car is a V12-powered Lincoln Zephyr.

Opposite: The Hammer Blow's interior is sheathed in varnished plywood, a favorite of do-it-yourselfers. The boxy design of the trailer made the construction and fitting of the interior elements much the same as those for a small cottage. Cooking was accomplished on a Coleman camping stove pictured on the right.

While trailer interiors of the late 1950s generally followed domestic trends, exterior styling was heavily influenced by the era's flamboyant automotive designs. Integrated two-tone paint schemes first appeared on cars during the early 1950s. By 1955, virtually every make offered two-tone or even three-tone paint jobs, usually defined by some form of rakish side trim. Wraparound windshields and backlights had also been widely adopted by 1955 and quickly became an emblem of automotive modernity. Trailer manufacturers did their best to echo such features after their own fashion: this 1957 Comet trailer, with its glass-cornered wraparound windshield and two-toned action lines, echoes the classic styling of the 1957 Chevrolet Bel Air tow car beyond.

Street seer Roger Babson, who predicted the stock market crash of 1929, forecast: "Within two decades one out of every two Americans will be living in a trailer." Babson's prediction never came to pass, but his prophetic statement added fuel to the mobile-America fire, so much so that by the end of the 1930s there were hundreds of companies manufacturing all shapes and sizes of travel trailers.

By then, these rolling bungalows had evolved far beyond Arthur Sherman's utilitarian box. Trailers came in all shapes and sizes, from tiny teardrop trailers that one needed to crawl into, to modest Canned Hams (so called because of their ovid shape), to lumbering mobile mansions with multiple bedrooms and rooftop balconies. Most of the trailers sported wood interiors that gave them the feel of a summer

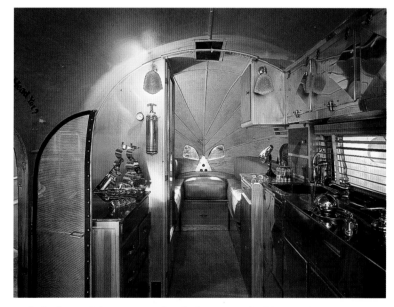

Even more vibrant interior colors arrived in the late 1950s, paralleling the fashion for vividly colored automobiles. The Comet features vinyl banquettes color-keyed to the laminated plastic panels in the cabinet doors, while the drain board uses a contrasting plastic laminate material edged in bright metal, as was customary until the early 1960s. The checkered floor and stove cover are a modern addition by the owner.

Polished metal, honey-toned upholstery, and ribbon mahogany paneling set an Art Deco mood in the interior of the Airstream. This view looks toward the rear sleeping quarters. The galley/kitchen is in the center of the trailer; a dining area is at the front. This trailer had air-conditioning, a rather modern convenience that was achieved by inserting a block of dry ice in a specially constructed chamber in the floor of the trailer.

cottage. Their tidy layout and their use of diminutive appliances only added to their charm.

Trailers, of course, needed to be parked somewhere, if only temporarily. So, both private landowners and municipalities hastily set up places for trailers to park. Many of these trailer parks evolved into cottage courts and, eventually, to motor hotels.

The travel trailer bubble finally burst at the beginning of the 1940s, but with an inevitable war looming on the horizon, the United States government knew that housing was going to be required around military bases for military personnel and civilian employees. The government turned to trailer manufacturers and commissioned thousands of "committee trailers," which were designed by a committee of three members appointed by the Trailer Coach Manufacturers Association. These trailers were not designed as recreational travel trailers but, rather, as portable homes. Because of their flimsy construction—wartime shortages of steel and aluminum forced manufacturers to substitute wood for framing,

Homosote for siding, and a painted canvas roof—few of these committee trailers survived.

The committee trailers fall under the broad umbrella of bread-loaf trailers. Because they were often larger and more house-like than other travel trailers, bread-loaf trailers were often marketed as cottages and vacation homes. Their popularity surged after World War II as America scrambled to provide housing for returning troops and their rapidly expanding families. Indeed, companies that manufactured airplanes during the war used the same technology to manufacture trailers. In 1948, less than three years after the war was over, more than 100,000 trailers were manufactured. The late 1940s and early 1950s were the golden age of the bread-loaf trailers. Sporting names like Vagabond, Westcraft, and Spartan—these elegant rolling homes, which were certainly more like cottages than travel trailers—had elegantly appointed interiors with all the latest appliances, wrapped in a durable aluminum skin. Today, people who seek to capture and celebrate a time when a modest and cozy home was good enough are lovingly restoring these finely crafted icons of America.

Opposite: In the past couple of decades, the trend in travel trailers has been big, bigger, and biggest. But there are manufacturers who still make modest-size trailers. Pictured is a 1972 Boler, designed by septic tank manufacturer Ray Oleko. The Boler's name comes from its resemblance to a bowler hat. Pictured with the trailer is a diminutive 1958 Nash Metropolitan.

chapter five

Enclaves

The concept of clusters of cottages is not a new one. Enclaves, in which buildings of similar style are built closely together, have often been used to enhance a sense of security and community. Religious organizations such as the Methodist Campground on Martha's Vineyard, founded in the 1830s and remodeled in the 1860s, grouped clusters of small Gothic cottages together, thus helping to foster the communal nature of their retreat. By the turn of the century, groups of small bungalow cottages, called "Bungalow Courts," were increasingly popular among architects and planners. The focus was

Kissimmee, Florida, c. 1980. Devoid of decoration, these cottages nonetheless are comfortable, with many multipaned windows to let the Florida sunshine stream in and small decks off the back to enjoy a cup of coffee and the morning paper.

A rustic lampshade made from seashells lights a table in the dining room. The owner collects lithographed nineteenth-century children's Christmas cards, a few of which are displayed behind the table.

Right: Onteora, New York, c. 1891. A rustic log gate and arbor lead into the garden surrounding this large cottage. The simple brown-shingled exterior and diamond-paned windows with red sashes are typical of the area's designs. Built for Mary Knight Wood, a woman composer who created the popular music entitled "Ashes of Roses" for the opening of the 1893 Chicago World's Fair, the home has musical references throughout its interior.

Opposite: Onteora, New York, 1893. Many of the Onteora cottages were simply constructed as just summer homes. Most did not have running water or heating other than fireplaces, and were used only during the summer and early autumn.

around a central courtyard, often with a fountain or garden. Bungalow courtyards helped provide a sense of intimacy and removal from the hustle and bustle of the world beyond their gates. Resort communities have continued to use this type of planning, and many summer retreats today feature groups of cottages built together.

By the 1920s, storybook-style housing was becoming more popular. Inspired by vernacular European farmhouses and villages, courtyards were made up of quaint half-timbered English cottages that looked straight out of the Cotswolds, but were in metropolitan America. Many thought Disney was inspired by some of these charming enclaves when buildings such as the Disney Court in Los Angeles, which was just down the road from the original movie studios, were built. Developers in other cities soon followed suit. In Alameda, just across the bay from San Francisco, Christopher Colombus Howard built several enclaves of picturesque detached houses. Charmingly clustered together in a U pattern, such as his 1927–29 courtyard called Stonehenge, Howard's developments were an oasis from the urban noise and traffic, and remain as popular today as when they were first built.

The Catskills of northern New York State had been a popular vacation destination since the early nineteenth century, and with the advent of the (Continued on page 132)

Onteora, New York, c. 1890. The back deck of this cottage features sweeping views of the Catskills. Notice the charming log railings. A gathering spot for early Onteora society, everyone from Samuel Clemens to Mrs. George A. Custer would visit during the summer.

Alameda, California, 1927–29. Stonehenge, the old English name that real estate developer Christopher Columbus Howard gave to his court-yard cottages, was meant to conjure up images of the English Cotswolds. Howard based his designs on plans published by Oakland architect Walter W. Dixon, one of the most prolific publishers in the 1920s of quaint storybook houses that employed "little features that suggest and give the character and feeling of the larger more expensive home." The entrance arch is built of richly colored Carmel chalkstone.

Alameda, California, 1927–29. Howard's design featured a group of detached cottages built in a U shape around a central courtyard. The moss-covered central stone fountain is still intact and accented by well-maintained plantings. This first development was so successful that Howard went on to build two adjacent similar courtyard enclaves, Stone Leigh in 1931 and Lincoln Court in 1941.

Los Angeles, California, 1919. One of the earliest storybook-style developments, Studio Court, was designed by Danish emigrant Einar Cortsen Petersen as a collection of artists' cottages. Meant to recall his native village of Abeltoft in Denmark, the unpretentious half-timbered cottages were built with a rustic look of heavy paneled doors, whitewashed walls, and irregular shake roofs, and faced a long, central paved courtyard. Petersen was a well-known artist in early Los Angeles; his murals were found in many buildings of the time. He developed these simple cottages as straightforward studios for his fellow artists and artisans.

Alameda, California, 1927–29. The two-story homes were thoughtfully planned so that driveways and garages were placed at the rear of each home, thus not obstructing views or access to the central courtyard. Cedar shake roofs accented by turrets, the liberal use of Carmel chalkstone in irregular patterns, and heavy wooden-plank entrance doors with large strap hinges all contribute to the handcrafted medieval look.

Los Angeles, California, c. 1927. This cluster of cottages is locally known as Disney Court, as it is very similar to the background of Walt Disney's 1937 film classic *Snow White and the Seven Dwarfs*. More recently, the cottages appeared in the David Lynch film *Mulholland Drive*. Neatly trimmed boxwood hedges; a moss-covered, curving, central brick pathway; simple whitewashed cottages accented by aged half-timbering; and irregular wood-shake roofs—it's easy to imagine you are truly in an English or German country village. How appropriate that the original telephone prefix for the area was "Ivanhoe," and even the developer was named Robert Sherwood.

Kissimmee, Florida, c. 1980. Florida has been booming as a resort destination since the 1930s as more people began to buy automobiles and travel farther afield for their holidays. In a re-creation of 1930s charm, these basic bungalettes were newly built off-site and brought in by trucks, spruced up in a rainbow of cheerful pastels, and readied to receive Aunt Selma and Uncle Sid. Money has not been wasted on extravagant plantings, as these have been built as an enclave of basic bungalows for middle-class families on vacation.

railroad by the middle of the century, summer resorts began to proliferate.

One such community, Onteora, was founded in the 1880s by well-known artist and author Candace Wheeler, and was built on a wooded mountain slope with sweeping views of the surrounding forests. Rustic wood-shingled cabins were constructed employing native materials such as birch logs and massive stone fireplaces. Meant originally for summer use only, these early enclaves were boarded up each fall as their occupants returned to their cities.

Enclaves often reflected the latest design trends. For example, one courtyard in California, the Egyptian Court, was built in the late 1920s in the exotic Egyptian Revival style, complete with concrete-and-bundled-papyrus pillars with hieroglyphic friezes.

Parrsboro, Nova Scotia, Canada, c. 1930. Cottages became increasingly popular as simple vacation homes beginning in the 1880s. Riverview Cottages are rare examples of an intact, well-preserved cottage court of the 1930s. These little houses were meant to be rustic and unadorned, intended as restful refuges from hectic urban lifestyles. They are still advertised as "No Television—No Telephone." Originally built for just $200 apiece, one of these cottages is still a very economical getaway, renting for only $35 dollars a night.

The tiny cottages are set on a scenic spot overlooking a lake amongst the evergreen trees. What could be more relaxing?

San Diego, California, 1926. Contractor Paul Carle built the exotic Egyptian Court Apartments in the Egyptian Revival style at the height of the Egyptian mania that swept the country in the 1920s following the discovery of King Tut's tomb. Massive concrete entrance pillars, flared at their tops, were meant to suggest bundled papyrus, while a frieze of marguerite daisies across the top was copied from a similar frieze across the Malkata Palace of Amenophis III (1342 b.c.) where King Tut was thought to have been born. The center decoration is of the sun god Ra, with cobras on each side and the wings of vultures spreading protectively outward. All of these exotic Egyptian decorations were readily available through local San Diego concrete manufacturers that advertised "period Egyptian ornamental stone."

The inner courtyard is built around a central pool, palm trees, and gardens, designed and installed by Milton P. Sessions, nephew of well-known San Diego horticulturist Kate Sessions, "the Mother of Balboa Park."

Detail of the entrance columns, which feature a hieroglyphic frieze of the goddess Hathor welcoming a pharaoh into the afterlife.

2854 - Flowers will grow like this for you in California —
on the Road of a Thousand Wonders - Southern Pacific

This 1906 southern Californian postcard portrays a bungalow court surrounded by colorful mounds of flowers—the good life in California as seen along the route of the Southern Pacific Railroad. The colors in these early postcards were applied over a black-and-white photograph by the printer in a process involving multiple printing plates.

Los Angeles, California, 1928. A small group of four cottages was designed by architect Allen Siple in 1928–29 for his own family; his wife and daughter lived in one until 1978, when the current owners bought the complex from Siple's daughter. Built around a central courtyard, each diminutive home has its own fireplace, mahogany hardwood floors and details such as beamed ceilings and knotty-pine paneling. These exterior stairs lead to a room above one of the garages and feature wishbone-style railings added by the current owners in true storybook-style whimsy.

Los Angeles, California, 1928. The living room is centered on a handsome fireplace that was hand-built with brick and roof tiles. Notice the original pine paneling to the left of the fireplace. The furniture is an eclectic blend of Art Deco pieces and several original Tiffany lamps.

The inviting breakfast nook still has its original corner cabinet. You can't help but begin your day in a bright mood after breakfast in this canary yellow room.

Los Angeles, California, 1928. The current owner built the door to his attic hideaway with antique stained glass, carved cherubs found at a flea market, and a rough wooden cross for an inviting rustic look.

Onteora, New York, 1893. Back in 1987, the homeowner of this cottage in the Catskills had never heard of Candace Wheeler, nor had anyone else. All she knew was that it was love at first sight when she saw the old cottage perched on (in fact, slowly sliding down) a mountain slope in a wooded enclave of rustic Victorian homes high in the Catskills. A massive stone fireplace, golden birch-bark railings, window seats, and plate rails in most of the rooms—how could she resist? No problem, she told her architect husband, that the entire house, never built as more than a simple summer retreat, needed to be jacked up and a new foundation poured to keep it from slipping down the mountain slope, or that the kitchen had to be torn apart, the floor taken up, and a giant rock removed that was pushing up through the center of the room (anything dropped in the room would swiftly roll into a dark corner).

The water coursing under the house could be easily rerouted with the right drainage, and the 1950s paint scheme of Williamsburg Blue just needed a fresh coat of a more sympathetic color. Just think of the house's charms, she explained to her spouse. The wide stone veranda would be a sunny spot for breakfast or a cozy retreat for a warm summer night's candlelit supper. The view across the Catskills from the upstairs bedrooms would be like waking up in a tree house. And even best, the house was being sold with its contents intact. The original aesthetic dining table and chairs were still in the dining room; mismatched but charming Arts and Crafts tables and chairs were scattered about beneath dust cloths; an enormous shabby old sofa, beckoning you to take a nap, rested in front of the great room's stone fireplace; and the clean and simple iron camp beds in the bedrooms were perfect for a refreshing night's sleep. All they really needed, she convincingly argued, were their toothbrushes.

The homeowner has a Ph.D. in art history, so it wasn't long before her curiosity was piqued and she began delving into her home's history. She soon learned that "some woman partner of Tiffany named Candace Wheeler" was an early founding member of the colony. Opened in 1888 by a wealthy real estate developer, the colony was given the name of Onteora, a local Indian name, and Candace Wheeler's son, Dunham, was the architect of many of the early cottages. Onteora soon became well known as an artists' retreat, for after Candace built her home, Pennyroyal, and began summering there, many of her famous friends followed. Samuel Clemens, better known as Mark Twain, was a frequent visitor; so was Mary Mapes Dodge, editor of *St. Nicholas Magazine;* General George A. Custer's widow, Elizabeth; and Maude Adams, J. M. Barrie's friend and the first Peter Pan. About 120 homes were built over the forested 1,600-acre mountaintop site over the next twenty years, all in a rustic vernacular style. Surprisingly, little changed after the turn of the nineteenth century. Used only as summer cottages, some fell or burned down over the years, but many survived. The great room is the heart of the cottage, soaring two stories and centered on a massive stone fireplace. Furnishings are a comfortable collection of family hand-me-downs, tag-sale finds, and original pieces left in the house.

A view of the dining room, showing the plate railing decorated with the owner's collection of brown-and-white transferware. Notice the eskewed angles of the walls, due to settlement of the house. The cottages in Onteora were never built very well, as they were meant as simple summer retreats, and most have significant settlement and problems such as frozen pipes in the winter—part of their rustic charm!

Golden birch logs frame the main staircase and lead past the original fir wainscoting to the second floor. The homeowner has filled the cottage with whimsical details, such as this stuffed rooster.

Aged fir wainscoting and ceiling give the dining room a warm and inviting glow. The room is centered on a stone fireplace that is decorated with a collection of tree fungi, some dating from the nineteenth century.

An upstairs bedroom is furnished simply with original brass beds and wicker furniture. The beadboard ceiling gives the room a warm glow.

chapter six

Contemporary Cottages

To be honest, it's not always easy to buy a cottage, even if you want one. Hard to find in cities with a scarcity of older neighborhoods, cottages are often located in urban or suburban areas that are not as fashionable as they once were. The logical choice for more and more people is to build their own cottage, a newer version of the classic design with all the advantages of the latest technology, located in a neighborhood of their choice. Everything from Victorian row houses to bungalow cottages—now being built in the style of their predecessors but firmly set in the twenty-first century—all have two elements crucial to the cottage mold: informality and charm.

This new, wee bungalette is nestled in a grove of trees on the Bay of Fundy in Nova Scotia, Canada. Vertical siding and an arched rustic-red front door add a touch of Gothic romance to this weekend getaway.

A brand-new bungalette rises in the Doe Mill subdivision in Chico, California. A traditional neighborhood is being created with modestly scaled bungalows that have popular details such as front bay windows, transoms above the doors, steeply pitched rooflines, and double-hung windows. Generous front porches and garages relegated to the rear of the homes help re-create the look of early-twentieth-century neighborhoods.

Hawaii has created heritage parks on two of its islands (Oahu and Maui), exhibiting historic cottages of early settlers. Oahu features plantation cottages in an enclave called Hawaii's Plantation Village. This cottage featured is called Portuguese House (1918). An outdoor museum, the village opened in 1992 to showcase the lifestyles and experiences of Hawaii's plantation workers who lived in these cottages from the late 1800s until the 1940s. Furnished homes and other community structures display and interpret the history of Hawaii's multiethnic heritage. Asian art and architecture, along with antiques and relics, are among the attractions of the village.

Like this Japanese duplex (1910) in Oahu, the simple, plantation workers' cottages featured wide porches to catch breezes, and simple, unadorned exteriors with vertical siding.

A small Japanese temple in Kepaniwai Heritage Gardens on Maui features an ornate, multi-gabled pagoda tile roof. A simple single room comprises the entire cottage, which becomes one with nature with its openness.

On Maui, a basic Hawaiian grass hut in Kepaniwai Heritage Gardens is built of stone with a steeply pitched, grass-covered roof. Surrounding the hut are taro plants, which are used to make poi, one of the staples of the Hawaiian diet.

Kepaniwai Heritage Gardens on Maui showcases exacting re-creations of historic cottages used by early settlers. This cottage is called a nipa hut, or Filipino range house, where a farmer lived close to his rice fields. The wide wraparound veranda offered a welcome refuge from the sun and frequent thunderstorms. The cottage is made of bamboo, with oak trees as posts and nipa leaves to cover the roof.

Robert Davis is a Florida businessman who spent idyllic childhood vacations on the Florida coast. When he inherited eighty acres on the northwest coast of Florida, he decided to re-create the memories of his childhood, and hired Miami architects Andres Duamy and Elizabeth Plater-Zyberk to help him. An old-fashioned community of wooden cottages emerged with deep overhanging eaves, tin roofs, ample windows, and cross-ventilation in all of the rooms. These cottages are laid out on picket-lined streets and squares, and people can comfortably walk to shop or dine. Some of the cottages are permanent homes, others are vacation getaways, and others can be rented by the night. Ecstasy, pictured here, is a cottage built in the tradition of Charleston, with the side facing the street. (This was done to decrease early taxation based on the footage of the house's front.) Tropical colors from turquoise to orange to purple give this cottage a whimsical appeal.

Telluride, Colorado, 1977. Called the Peach House by locals, this whimsical gingerbread gem built by Jack Para follows the fanciful designs of a local artist. Carved flowers embellish the gables, which are accented by a handsome turret. Telluride has been a historic landmark since 1964, and this new Victorian beauty blends in seamlessly.

This reborn Victorian located in Redondo Beach, California, was a simple 1880s cottage before the owner decided to embellish it a little. Beginning in 1978, he added a tower, another octagonal bay, an extension to the back of the home, and even a second story. Every Victorian detail was added, from a patterned shingled roof, to decorative spindles and porch railings, to ornate cresting and finials on the towers and roof.

Los Angeles, California, 1932. This enclave of storybook-style cottages was designed by Allen Siple, a Los Angeles architect. Built on a courtyard design, they survived until the 1980s, when they were threatened with demolition for new construction. In 1988 the developers relocated the cottages to a nearby site and completely rebuilt them for use as offices. Attention to detail during reconstruction ensured the cottages' personality was kept intact. This cottage is centered on an imposing turret, and a tiny second-story balcony adds to its storybook charm.

Opposite: A rustic wishing well is the focal point of this section of the courtyard. The "tree trunks" are actually wire-reinforced concrete. A vintage-style street lamp adds to the ambience.

Opposite, right: Another cottage in the enclave is covered with rambling ivy in the time-honored English tradition. The grounds were professionally landscaped and the cottages sited among trees and English-style gardens bordered by boxwood hedges. Wooden shutters and mullioned windows add to the old-world charm.

The Grove, as this Los Angeles complex was named, centers around a picturesque paved courtyard that shuts out noise and makes it easy to forget the hustle and bustle of everyday life beyond its gates.

This new Victorian cottage in Seaside, Florida, is aptly named The Dollhouse. Projecting bays on either side and corner quoins accent the nineteenth-century look. The house is painted in a soft pastel palette, perfect for the tropical Florida coast.

Opposite: The Cottage of the Future could be the name for this unique Del Mar, California, home built in the 1980s by architect James Hubbell. Nestled in a grove of eucalyptus trees, the organic forms are centered on two domes intersected by a tiled patio. Built for a writer of mystery books, the home uses a combination of outdoor and indoor spaces in its free-flowing design. The domes were ingeniously formed with large balloons that were sprayed with concrete and then deflated. A white plaster finish gives a Mediterranean feel to this futuristic cottage. The interior features undulating surfaces and is accented with mosaic tiles and stained-glass windows. This is not a house for everyone, as the architect cautions, and needs to fit the individual much like a good shoe.

The living room glows from the light of a stained-glass panel in the center of the box-beamed ceiling. The massive fireplace, influenced by Scottish designer Charles Rennie Mackintosh, still seems modern with its design of simple curves. The unusual iron fireplace grate was made by Eric Clausen and is accented by an Arts and Crafts–style copper-and-brass fender by Michael Bondi. Oak furniture by Limbert includes a settle, rocking chair, and round library table.

Opposite: The master bedroom features a stylized floral frieze inspired by Mackintosh, utilizing the Glasgow rose, one of his favorite motifs. The curtains were designed and sewn by the owners. A Liberty of London dressing table (not in the picture) was used as inspiration for the newly constructed bed and night tables.

This new bungalow cottage pays homage to the best of the English Arts and Crafts movement, with sinuous stained-glass windows, a medieval paneled-oak front door and surround, and a substantial entry gable. Sited on a steep hillside in San Francisco, the house opens onto the main living area, with stairs leading down to the bedrooms, a library, and a garden terrace.

Firefighter Richey Morgan has been building his own version of a storybook cottage for the past twenty years in the rural Washington town of Olalla. Straight out of Hansel and Gretel, sinuous walls and gables beckon the visitor across a small stream to the front door.

The interior is as unique as the exterior. Handcrafted planks carved with a chain saw and belt sander form the stairs leading to the attic bedroom. The arch dividing the kitchen from the dining room is carved out of a five-foot-diameter cedar tree trunk.

Opposite: The exaggerated rooflines are the perfect showplace for the seawave shingled roof and rolled eaves. Notice the overscaled front door's strapwork hinges and door-knocker—straight out of a fairy tale. The owners handcrafted everything. The 300-pound door was made with a chain saw, belt sander, and steady hand.

Resources

Whether you have a storybook-style château from the 1920s or a newly built bungalette, finding just the right craftspeople to restore and maintain your home with sensitivity to its design is crucial. The following is a list, by no means all-inclusive, of some of our favorite craftspeople and manufacturers. We have divided our guide into six major categories of restoration, e.g. Kitchens, Baths, Walls and Ceilings, Furnishing Details, Lighting, and Hardware.

Kitchens

Kennebec Company: kennebeccompnay.com. Period-inspired cabinetry from Colonial to early 20th century, handcrafted in Maine, using authentic joinery and details. (207) 443-2131

Crown Point Cabinetry: crown-point.com. Hand-crafted custom cabinetry in period-inspired styles, with a variety of finishes including Old-Fashioned Milk Paint. (800) 999-4994

Ashfield Stones. Exclusive quarries of stones unique to the Berkshires, custom stonework from sinks and countertops to fireplaces. (413) 628-4773

AA Abbingdon Affiliates: abbingdon.com. Original tin ceilings and walls in steel, copper, brass, white and chrome. (718) 258-8333

Green Mountain Soapstone: greenmountainsoapstone.com. Precision-crafted soapstone sinks, flooring tiles as well as slabs for custom installation. (802) 468-5636

Elmira Stove Works: elmirastoveworks.com. Cast-iron, nickel-trimmed Victorian cook stoves with modern conveniences. (800) 295-8498

Antique Appliances: antiqueappliances.com. Restores all makes of antique refrigerators and stoves and maintains a large inventory of restored appliances for sale. (706) 782-3152

Baths

Birdseye Building Company: birdseyebuilding.com. Handcrafted, custom-designed vanities and built-ins in styles from Arts and Crafts to contemporary. (802) 434-2112

Clawfoot Supply: clawfootsupply.com. Supplier of historic and reproduction fixtures for period bath restorations.

Web Wilson: webwilson.com. Good selection of antique tubs, sinks, toilets and bath accessories from towel bars to mirrors. (800) 508-0022

Bathroom Machineries: deabath.com. Early American and Victorian bathroom fixtures and fittings, antique and reproduction. (209) 728-2031

Mac the Antique Plumber: antiqueplumber.com. Extensive variety of antique and reproduction plumbing and accessories. (800) 916-BATH

Walls and Ceilings

Derby Pottery and Tile: derbypottery.com. Hand-pressed and finished reproduction tile for fireplaces, backsplashes, tubs and showers. (504) 586-9003

Charles Rupert Designs: charles-rupert.com. Reproductions tiles, wallpapers and fabrics in English and American Arts and Crafts and Victorian styles. (250) 592-4916

L'Esperance Tile. Hand-pressed porcelain tiles in many historic designs. (518) 884-2814

Epoch Designs: epochdesigns.com. Authentic Victorian stencils (610) 565-9180

Benjamin Moore Paints: benjaminmoore.com. Quality paints since 1883, the Historic Color Collection offers interior and exterior period appropriate paints. (800) 344-0400

JR Burrows &Co.: burrows.com. Arts and Crafts wallpapers, fabric, carpet and lace curtains. (800) 347-1795

Carol Mead Designs: carolmead.com. Hand-printed wallpapers, borders and friezes in British and American turn-of-the-century patterns. (707) 747-0223

Bradbury and Bradbury Art Wallpapers: bradbury.com. Hand silk-screened papers in Neoclassical, Victorian and Arts and Crafts styles. (707) 746-1900

Trustworth Studios: trustworth.com. Period home restoration specializing in English Arts and Crafts in the spirit of C.F.A. Voysey. (508) 746-1847

Furnishing Details

Joan Bogart Antiques: joanbogart.com. American lighting and furniture from 1820 to 1900. (516) 764-5712

Southhampton Antiques: southamptonantiques.com. Large selection of American antiques. (413) 527-1022

L and JG Stickley: stickley.com. Reissues of original designs of the Stickleys and Harvey Ellis. (315) 682-5500

Warren Hile Studio: hilestudio.com. Hand crafted Mission furniture. (626) 359-7210

Ann Wallace and Friends: annwallace.com. Arts and Crafts curtains made to order in natural fibers, also pillows and table runners. (213) 617-3310

Scalamandré: scalamandre.com. Traditional and historic textiles, trimmings and wallpapers. (800) 932-4361

Archive Edition Textiles: archiveedition.com. Fine woven fabrics in Arts and Crafts designs. (877) 676-2424

Lighting

Antique Lighting Company: antiquelighting.com. Reproductions of antique light fixtures in a wide array of styles and finishes. (800) 244-7800

Rejuvenation: rejuvenation.com. Over 500 lighting styles and hard-to-find house parts. (888) 401-1900

Michael Ashford Evergreen Studios: evergreenstudios.com. Arts and Crafts chandeliers and lamps with hand-hammered copper and mica glazing. (360) 352-0694

Omega Too: omegatoo.com. Unique antique and reproduction lighting and plumbing. (510) 843-3636

Hardware

Eugenia's Antique Hardware: eugeniaantiquehardware.com. Authentic antique hardware, no reproductions. (800) 337-1677

Crown City Hardware: restoration.com. Extensive antique hardware reproductions from the 17th thru the early 20th century. (800) 950-1047